# MY LIFE'S CIRCLE

# My Life's Circle

## A Boy's Dream Comes True

TERRY BODINE

Terry Bodine

# CONTENTS

I wish to thank my daughter Miranda and
sister Brenda for their willingness to lend
me a hand, both in life and with this book.
I love you both.

First Printing, 2020

# PREFACE

I grew up on a cash crop farm in western New York. My father was once the largest farmer in our county, working close to 2,500 acres between land he owned and that which he leased. He was also a grain dealer, planting and purchasing assorted grains we would later truck with ten-wheelers.

As a teenager during the late '60s and early '70s, my help on the family farm was not asked for but expected. Sleepless nights were frequent, as I transitioned from student to field hand the moment I got home from school, often until three in the morning. My involvement was pivotal to our family's prosperity. I was the hinge pin.

In 1970, my father took a call from a nearby John Deere dealer. They had a four-wheel drive, articulated tractor which a local farmer had ordered, but failed to purchase. They wondered if he might be interested? A 7020 John Deere, it would be the first and most prominent of its kind to break ground in our area. Curious, Dad told the dealer to bring the tractor by the farm, and if his son (me) could handle it, he'd buy it. Several days had elapsed before it arrived on sight. Ol' Moe, as we would affectionately name it years later, was massive. John Deere green and shiny clean, it shadowed everything parked beside it. The salesman rode beside me for several rounds until he was comfortable with my performance. Well pleased with its power and my ability behind the wheel, Dad purchased the tractor for $20,000. By comparison, a tractor of the same size today would easily cost $200,000. I can still remember the

30-acre field I plowed that day and the tilled earth which lay in my wake. The tractor and I were nearly inseparable for the following two years.

It was my father's involvement in the grain industry, which first sparked my interest in trucks. The ten-wheelers he had were all red fords, he insisted on both the make and color. At harvest time, I would move them from field to field for loads, always staying close to home since I didn't have my chauffeur's license. Despite my mother's caution and constant worry, I managed this task for over two years without ever getting pulled over by law enforcement, thank God!

We always worked hard and ate well, growing up on the farm. On weekends Dad would wake my brother and me up at 4 am to start our day. You could always smell breakfast cooking as you made your way downstairs. The aroma might be trout, caught by one of his buddies, pork chops, hamburgers, or even fresh pig or beef liver. Aside from being a cash crop farm, we also raised livestock for the market, so beef and pork were readily available. While it was Dad who had the breakfast shift, all other meals fell to my mother, who could be counted upon to feed the family, and often the hired help. She also ran a fresh fruit and vegetable stand in front of our home. It was known to have some of the best sweet corn and homemade pies around. Mom ran that stand with the help of my younger sister for a good 25 years and always did remarkably well.

The farm dictated which sport I might play while in high school. Spare time was unheard of during either planting or harvest seasons. Fortunately, my love was and still is basketball. I was part of many good teams through the years, and although we'd make finals every year, we could never quite win a championship. My folks were perhaps my biggest fans, traveling to and from away games, as well as those held at home, I always appreciated their unwavering support.

Time passed, and before I knew it, I was soon a senior in high school, contemplating what to do with my life. Despite being both a regents and honor roll student, I had no desire to attend college, or be far from home. I was in love with my high school sweetheart and hoped to marry her soon after graduation. I considered two career paths, and both offered me the opportunity to be the boss. I would either start a construction or trucking business, but which?

As acres churned beneath me, perhaps guided by Ol' Moe's exhaust stack, by summers end I had chosen to give trucking a try. I talked things over with my father, and together we purchased the first of several trucks. It's there that my story begins.

# ~ 1 ~

# THE BEGINNING

It was the summer of 1972, and I had just graduated from high school. I was trucking wheat to a village in Central New York, with one of my father's ten-wheelers. While at a grain mill, I ran into a farmer who was driving a red Ford ten-wheeler, which was identical to the one I was driving. In truth, it was in much better shape and only had 15,000 miles on it. It was a 1966 Ford with a V8 gas motor and a twenty-foot body, complete with a lift and 5-foot sides. In conversation, I learned that this old farmer was ready to retire, so I asked him how much he would take for his truck. He thought about it for a while and then gave me the figure of $7,500. This truck was only six years old and hardly driven. I came home and excitedly told my father and fiance what I hoped to do. Convinced I was crazy, they were quick to dismiss my thoughts as adventurous and unaffordable. My dream and I were benched.

In 1974, I married my high school sweetheart. A year later, I was the father of a bright-eyed little girl. Though my family was doing great, my career was going nowhere fast. My love for trucks remained ever-present. I just needed a chance to make things happen. Little did I know that while camping in Watkins Glen, NY, some 40 miles from my home, a chance meeting would soon set my dreams in motion.

I was barbecuing chicken at our campsite when a stranger approached me and commented on how good the chicken was smelling. We stood there for a few minutes and just talked about life in general. The more I spoke to this man, the more I felt I knew him from somewhere. I invited him and his wife to stop over after dinner for a cocktail. As I only had vodka to offer as a beverage, he brought his bottle of gin. We partied and played euchre for half the night. It was driving me crazy that I couldn't place this fellow. I kept asking him questions, hoping to recall where we'd met. He told me he was a farmer that grew potatoes and wheat in Churchville, N.Y. As we grew grains as well, he asked if I had ever been to the flour mill in Churchville. A dim light (½ bottle of vodka later) came on. This gentleman was the same man who offered to sell his 1966 Ford ten-wheeler to me two years earlier! My heart was pounding as I asked him if he still owned the ten-wheeler I'd fallen in love with, not so long ago. To my amazement, he did and offered me the chance to purchase it yet again. I laugh still today, knowing that our signatures upon a paper napkin had closed the deal. I bought his truck that night for $6,000 sight unseen. We shook hands, and I said I would deliver his money the following week when I picked up the truck.

The next morning, my wife looked straight into my bloodshot eyes and stated, "Where the hell are you going to get $6,000?" I knew I couldn't afford this truck on my own, but if I could convince my father, maybe, just maybe. With high hopes and a hangover, I walked into my father's office the next day and revealed my plan. He thought I was crazy (notice that will be a trend), but softened some, agreeing to cosign a loan for me.

As my wife and I set off for Churchville, with money in my pocket, I began second-guessing myself. Who buys a truck they haven't driven or even seen in two years? Now in debt for $6,000 with a young family looking to me for support and care. Holy shit, what had I done?

My fears vanished as I pulled into the farmer's driveway. There it sat, a beauty for sure, just the way I remembered. That truck never let me down; for four years, she hauled grapes, vegetables, and grain. Other than regular maintenance, I never had to put a dime into it.

Soon, our business was growing, and our need for larger trucks became inevitable. Needing to sell my first truck, I painted its deck and racks black, then parked it out front with a sign asking $15,000. I didn't care if it sold or not, I still loved that truck and the story that came with it.

A few weeks went by before a couple of loggers stopped to look the truck over. They offered me $14,000 but I turned it down, suggesting that for their price, I would only take cash. They walked away, calling me crazy for not considering their offer. It was never about the money; the purchase of the truck had been my first step in starting my own business, and it had sentimental value. As luck or good fortune would have it, the loggers returned the following week and handed me 140, one hundred dollar bills. It made me sad, watching that truck pull away, its taillights fading in the distance. It was the first and only time in my forty years of buying and selling vehicles, that I would sell one for such a profit.

# ~ 2 ~

# THE WHEELS START TO TURN

Purchasing that 1966 Ford ten-wheeler was just the break I needed, it helped to establish roots in a business that would grow beyond my highest expectations. Next, Dad and I bought a new 1974 International cab over, with a 318 Detroit engine and a new 28' Tibrook dump trailer. Our one dilemma, neither of us had our Class A. I wasted no time in obtaining my permit, followed soon after by my license. Dad followed suit, and together our business spawned.

As the demand for our services grew, so did the number of trucks and trailers we owned. I was hauling both grains from Dad's farm, as well as grain he would purchase on the open market. We soon added a used 1974 Ford Louisville and a new 1975 Ford Louisville, both with 318 Detroit engines to our fleet. We quickly realized that we would need additional help if we planned to keep the wheels turning and the money coming in. In 1977 as we purchased yet another new Ford Louisville with a 350 Cummins engine, I began interviewing new drivers to help carry the load. Farming and trucking were flourishing, and I was in the driver's seat, doing what I had planned to do.

During those early years, we bought a used single axle Brockway with a 250 Cummins engine, for use as a yard horse around the farm. Though it was an oldie, it was a goodie. Having cost $2500, the old girl more than carried her share of loads. Ever short on trucks, it could be counted upon without worry, more than once going clear to Albany, NY, over 200 miles away without issue.

# ~ 3 ~

# ALL HELL BROKE LOOSE

In the Fall of 1977, my father had a massive shop/storage building constructed. The shop area was heated and could hold four tractors and trailers parked side by side. The other half of this 150' by 60' building served as a storage unit for both equipment and grain. This building provided us the space and convenience that a growing business needed to maintain both daily operations and a leg up on the competition.

The following winter brought the unexpected to our family business. We woke one morning to find that the entire roof of the new barn had collapsed. The burden of heavy snow, which had fallen overnight, had proven too much for the newly constructed barn to bear. A bad situation made worse, as the shop had been full of trucks, and my folks first and only motorhome. The storage unit held the balance of 25 trailer loads of wheat awaiting market.

We first hired a crane to pick the barn roof off from the trucks. The cabs were impaled with 2 x 6 lumber, resulting from the speed and weight of the collapse. Each eventually sent to a body shop for windshield replacements and repairs to their cabs. The tools located in the shop were the next to be retrieved, followed by the 25 loads of wheat stored in the back part of the barn, which had to be reloaded and dried before being sold at the market. As expenses continued to climb, we debated whether to resurrect the current building or begin from scratch on a new structure.

Efforts to recover money from the contractor who built the original structure were in vain. Having sought protection through bankruptcy, the builder relinquished his ownership of a rusted out pickup truck as court-ordered compensation to my father and not a dime more. Determined to move forward, Dad found a contractor that would straighten the walls and put a new roof on the existing barn, who was willing to guarantee his work. With one building standing, at the cost of two, $200,000 in the hole, we were back up and running.

# ~ 4 ~

# LIFE REINVENTED

In 1978, my wife and I now have two daughters. Though still living in a mobile home, we were financially stable. Eager to complicate our already busy lives, we decided to purchase a piece of property in the Finger Lakes, where an old gas station stood erect. We remodeled it and slowly turned it into a fruit and vegetable stand. Though located about 20 miles from our residence, it was just around the corner from my wife's mother and sibling brothers. We bought the property, intent on selling sweet corn that we grew on our farm.

My wife, also an entrepreneur, made this her baby. The 25 acres of sweet corn which we planted, could now be sold retail at our new stand. It didn't take long before selling out of corn became a daily event. Our produce soon became a staple for seasonal cottagers, sprinkled up and down the nearby lake and State Park.

Quickly assessing the volume of daily traffic, location, and the economics of supply and demand, my wife concluded that our little stand was falling short of its potential. After making significant improvements, our produce market reopened, featuring an assortment of fruits and vegetables, in full swing from Memorial Day until Labor Day, seven days a week. I was managing a sweet corn crew of ten pickers from mid-July through late August, all while keeping the trucking business alive and flourishing.

In 1980, we purchased a small camper to be placed behind the produce market. This became the second home for my wife, two daughters, and a son born in June. With the unending help of her family, our business thrived.

Twice a week, my wife would head out for the Regional Market in Syracuse, NY, at three in the morning. She would load my pickup to its capacity, with produce for our stand. With business exploding, by the third year, I was building racks for my truck so we could haul even more. Still not enough, during our fifth year of business, we invested in a 12' trailer to tow behind the bed of my pickup. It was then that I took over going to the market twice a week, in addition to managing a sweet corn crew, and the operations of our trucking business. Still unable to meet demand, I eventually purchased an Isuzu diesel truck with a 14' cube refrigerated body.

We continued to expand that fruit stand until it didn't look anything like the little ol' gas station it had once been. More land was purchased to provide a bigger parking lot for our patrons. We added an ice cream parlor, equipped with two unique blending machines capable of combining fruit with ice cream, and a pastry kitchen to permit the baking of fresh pies, cookies, and loaves of bread. We even tried our hand at operating a greenhouse, hoping to sell perennials and annuals.

We operated that stand for 28 years, employing countless high school students along the way. My daughters would take charge and help my wife and I manage the daily needs of running the fruit stand. My son, no longer a child, would accompany me to the Regional Market, helping to purchase our produce.

By the time we sold, the market had twenty-three employees on the payroll. Looking back, I have no idea how we had the energy to run both businesses, alongside growing sweet corn. All I know is that it was a great time. I will long cherish the memories and the people that helped make the stand, the success that it was.

# ~ 5 ~

# THE FIRST OF MANY

Two years following our purchase of the little ol' gas station, while hauling grapes to Northeast PA, I kept driving past this Peterbilt dealership. A long nose Peterbilt with a 475 Detroit engine kept catching my eye. She was a beauty, with brown and orange striping down her long white frame. I had to have it. The salesman said that a down payment of $5000 would be enough to hold the truck of my dreams. I left Pennsylvania that day knowing what my next step had to be.

Once again, I looked towards dear old Dad for some help with this transaction. I went back to PA. the following week with another load of grapes and Dad's credit card in my pocket. The truck had it all, big horsepower, lots of chrome, and a 250" wheelbase. When Dad and I arrived to pick up the Peterbilt, he couldn't believe how gorgeous it was. He was equally surprised to see my name proudly painted on its visor. I figured that if I was going to do the majority of the trucking, then why not put my name somewhere visible. In my opinion, it was the sharpest truck we ever owned, I finally felt like I was moving forward with my life.

# ~ 6 ~

# GOING NUTS

With summer behind us, the fruit stand closed for the season and fall approaching, our trucks and drivers enjoyed the final push of the year. Assorted varieties of grapes, destined for area wineries, were ready to be harvested and hauled. As the family farm also held acreage in both Concord and Niagara strands, we would close out the year running loads of grapes, our own included, to many wine producers.

Not long after purchasing the Peterbilt and with the arrival of winter, trucking had begun to slow, as could be anticipated for that time of year. With business down, Dad accepted a round trip deal, which involved a good payout. We decided to go for it.

The venture involved loading television components in Geneva, NY, destined for California. After three stops, we would catch a predetermined load back to Geneva, NY. The job screamed easy money, requiring a reliable truck, (mine) and two responsible drivers who could work together as a team. It seemed like a no-brainer. We had two young drivers that were both capable and willing to make the trip. To make the experience more enticing, I was allowing the drivers to utilize my Pete, what could go wrong? In honesty, cross country trips had never been in our wheelhouse, as to say, most of our work was local or within a few hundred miles.

The drivers were both excited to go. Neither of them had ever been to the west coast. The best of companions here to home, we had no worries that they wouldn't make a great trip team going forward. They polished my truck inside and out for two days. Though family needs kept me from going, I sure wish I had. My rig looked terrific, with all its chrome sparkling, adventure awaited.

Dad visited the bank and pulled out $3000 cash for fuel and expenses for the boys. Back then, drivers always carried cash instead of credit cards. It should have been more than enough for the trip, expected to last just seven days.

Dad and I drove a car over to Geneva, NY. to see the guys off. Shaking hands, saying, "Be safe, we'll see you in a week." With drop times scheduled, the trip was to be a walk in the park. Or not.

After two and a half days of travel, the boys arrived in California. They called to report that all was running according to plan. The "Pete," was performing tremendous, and they planned on making all the scheduled appointments. It's here that I interject, reminding folks that while CB radios were ever popular for short-range chatter, cell phones were scant and ill-prepared for use on the highway. With that said, the only time we would hear from the drivers was when they chose to call. Their phone call home expounding upon the trip west was the last we would hear from them until fifteen days later, when they found themselves flat broke in Cleveland, OH.

Unbeknownst to us, the boys had determined their pending trip home dictated they celebrate in sunny California while the opportunity presented itself. Their plan, as I understood it, was to make it to the last stop, unload, but not reload until they'd made time for some sightseeing all while using my truck and our cash!

Days went by, without a word from either driver. Then a week passed by without sight of the big-rig, or the sound of its air horn announcing their arrival home. Week two came and went, with one exception. On the final day, two weeks following their departure, the telephone in my father's office rang. After several minutes listening to my Dad purge himself of profanity, in desperation, they began pleading their well-rehearsed case. Contrived or not, they suggested that another trucking company had stolen their load. (because they were late for the appt.). The next shipment for Geneva, NY. was a month out. They had done their level best to find a return load, eventually taking a load of walnuts destined for Ohio. By the time they had made it there, they had used all our cash, and their own, on fuel, gambling at the casinos, drinking and just plain raising hell.

The hot load we ventured would make us great money, had gone to shit! We had to wire the boys more money just to see the truck make it home, with a last-minute load we'd scrambled to get in Ohio.

When the Peterbilt finally rolled itself into the driveway, it had been nearly three weeks since its departure. The boys' names had been changed without their knowledge, replaced by others, the least offensive being, "clowns." When the ass-chewing ended, our losses totaled, we quickly concluded that we wouldn't be an over the road trucking company. We kept the "clowns" on because they were good at what they did. With time, Dad cut them some slack, and we all developed a good working relationship.

The following winter, as if on cue, my father and I agreed to a long-distance run from New York, to somewhere in Texas.

Though both drivers were eager to go as a team, the California Ka-bobble rang clear in heads. We quickly dismissed the notion, sending just one of the "clowns" instead.

# ~ 7 ~

# FEELING THE SQUEEZE

By the mid-1980s, interest rates were going through the roof, and everyone was feeling the impact. My wife and I were seeing less profit from the trucking business each week, while still trying to feed our family of five. It was nearly impossible to live on $250.00 a week and manage everyday needs. I couldn't believe how fast things went downhill. Making matters worse, the 475 Detroit engine in my Pete had just blown up.

My folk's farm was in peril. My father's farming expenses and spending habits had outpaced our joint earnings. The situation demanded he auction off some of his farm equipment and trucks. Forever my father's son, the end of our mutual business endeavor, had been reached. With my beloved Pete on the chopping block, my wife and children's needs paramount; I ventured forward on my own.

The Detroit representatives in Syracuse, NY, stood behind the defective motor and would pay half the cost of installing a new 475 Detroit engine. I had a friend haul the old motor out, and we placed the Pete up for bidding, without a motor in it.

I couldn't bring myself to be at Dad's auction. The farm had become a noose I was no longer willing to wear, nor one my family and I could afford any longer. My father's temperament had changed, as well. Perhaps in envy of my growing success and newfound independence, his silence resonated his concern for the farm's future.

A buddy of mine attended the auction, in my absence. I instructed him, come hell or high water to be the highest bidder on my Pete, thankfully he was.

## ~ 8 ~

# ON THE ROAD AGAIN

Having purchased the Pete back for $15,000 and spent another $7,500 to replace the motor, at ½ the cost, the wheels were turning once again. I managed to connect with a broker in Buffalo, NY, hauling wooden posts to Long Island, while catching return loads from the docks in New Jersey. Three round trips each week, made for substantial earnings. Though seldom home, financially, things were looking up. Now independent, I alone was in charge of our destiny.

It was around this time that we sold our mobile home, relocating to a raised ranch style house several towns to the east. The move enabled me to connect with Agway, an abundant agricultural supply and marketing cooperative spanning 13 states along the east coast. As my involvement with Agway grew, so did my trucking of their fertilizers and grains. It was a dream come true. Soon, past troubles were distant memories. I was networking and building relationships with Agway employees, from the top on down. I became terrific friends with the managers of the smaller stores. Agway was continuing to grow, and I needed to grow with them. Life began to mirror my youthful aspirations.

I started investing in my own business. I was buying trucks and trailers for my fleet. My first purchase was a new 1988 International sleeper with a 550 CAT engine. Next, came a used 1990 International with the same engine. In the years 1995 through 1999, I added five more used Peterbilts to the fleet, ever grateful for their reliability.

It should come as no surprise that in 2000 I found myself purchasing a brand new Pete. My wife and I were heading off to New Hampshire for a little get-a-way, mixed with a stop or two at some dealerships. We stopped at a Peterbilt franchise near I 90 in Utica, NY. After looking over the inventory and speaking with a sales associate, I was ready to move on, when my eyes caught a stunning maroon colored Pete coming out of the wash bay. I immediately pulled back into the parking lot and found a salesman. Unwilling to spend more than $100,000, by the end of that day, I was the proud owner of a maroon Peterbilt. We never made it to New Hampshire. Instead, we found ourselves home by nightfall. Reflecting, I cut that romantic weekend short and should have praised my wife for never saying a word about it.

The business was going better than I could imagine. In 2002 I went back to the same dealership in Utica and walked away with two more Peterbilts with 550 CAT engines under my name. I gave the salesman the same parameters as I had before. Unwilling to spend over $100,000 for either truck, he conceded.

By this time, I was running dump trailers, tankers, flatbeds, walking floors, vans, and even a few refrigerated trailers. I was still driving, as well as dispatching my employees, a task made easy through association with some exceptional friends at Agway.

# ~ 9 ~

# TOO MANY EGGS IN ONE BASKET

My life has had its share of ups and downs. Once, while on top of my "A" game, I learned that Agway had gone broke. The news was devastating. Agway had served as our sole source of income. I had invested hundreds of thousands of dollars into my business based upon my growing relationship with them. I had incurred particular debts, knowing that my business, now an LLC, was stable. My drivers, including my younger brother, who hauled for me as an independent contractor, feared for their future. I was 50 years old and scared shitless, what the hell do I do?

Back to the drawing board, I went. With a family to support and three young adults venturing to college, I knew that propelling myself forward was the only direction to take. My first step in figuring this whole mess out, required I remove myself from the trucks and work solely from my office, a road I was unaccustomed to taking.

# ~ 10 ~

## RE-BUILDING MY FUTURE

The first few years after Agway went under were the roughest of my career. I reached out to Agway's competition, in hopes of getting my foot in the door. Work was slim in the beginning, but I was able to keep all of my employees and the wheels moving. Perseverance paid off, but I am thankful every day for my wife's deep faith and the banking arrangements we made at the start. When I decided to go out on my own, after my father's bankruptcy, I arranged with my bank to make yearly payments on the business loans. That way, I could have a few bad months and still make my payment at the end of the year. In my 40 years of business, we never missed a payment, my wife handled that end of the company, and I am grateful for her common sense and tenacity. There is a good woman behind every successful man, at least in my case. I couldn't have made it through this journey without her.

The work was back on track. I was hauling for many different companies, rather than one. With phone calls to make and loads to schedule, I seldom spent time out of the office. Dispatching loads to and from, amongst multiple entities, guaranteed a daily headache but ensured I would never find myself in the same predicament again.

As I reflect on the pros and cons of working with Agway, I would be remiss if I didn't acknowledge having loved every minute of it. When Agway folded its doors, they still owed me $12,000. I figured that I would never see that money and chalked it up to the cost of doing business. I was sad to see the company dissolved. Perhaps out of gratitude, their loyalty, the many friends I'd made along the way, I never sought an attorney to collect the debt.

One of my closest friends from Agway, called me a few months after the news had gone public. He informed me to gather up any bills that Agway still owed me, and send them to him directly. Almost a year from the date of that conversation, I received a check for the full amount. I still miss the Agway years and the acquaintances that I made along the way.

# ~ 11 ~

## TOO GOOD TO BE TRUE

Over the 40 years of being in the trucking business, I have hired many, many drivers. I suppose, a little arrogance began to grow on my part, as I believed I could read applicants pretty well, before hiring them on. I couldn't have been more wrong.

One afternoon a stranger stopped by the office and proceeded to tell me his life's story. I informed this new acquaintance right from the start that I wasn't looking for any new drivers. This man was captivating and easy to talk with, so I let him continue. I learned that he was originally from Maryland, where he and his brother owned a chain of funeral homes left to them by their father. After the death of one of his children, emotionally unable to continue operating the family business, he and his brother agreed to sell out. His brother had invested his money into breeding racing horses all over the world, while the young man sitting in my office, wanted to buy a trucking business. He planned to immerse himself in the industry until he felt he could go it alone. Goal-oriented, his intentions had garnered my interest, as my wife and I had shared conversations, contemplating retirement. After spending a couple of hours with this stranger, taken by his honesty, sure he was someone I could trust, and without reservation, I offered him the chance to come aboard.

This new employee had a great attitude and would take trips that other drivers refused. He never said no or whined about the type of work I gave him. He lived close to our business, which allowed him to be readily available anytime. I continued to enjoy our conversations and felt that our future held endless possibilities.

I have learned through this experience and countless others that if something appears too good to be true, it probably is. Six months after hiring my star employee, I got a phone call from Federal Marshals in Maryland. They were looking for my new hire and wanted to know how much I knew about him. These guys meant business, and the very next day, they were at my office wanting to know when he was expected back. When my answers didn't give the authorities what they needed, they contacted the driver's girlfriend, and the race was on!

Hoping to set up a roadblock and arrest him on the spot, I convinced them to let him pull into my truck lot without causing a big scene. He was expected home that day from New Jersey, and everything should have fallen right into place. The problem with this scenario, the girlfriend had tipped him off. He never came back to my truck lot. He turned off the cell phone and was running scared with my truck and a trailer load of frozen orange juice.

These Marshals could care less about my truck, it was him they wanted. The New York State Police wouldn't even start looking for my rig for at least fourteen days. I then contacted my local sheriff's department, and to my surprise and disappointment, I received the same news from the deputy standing in my office. My blood pressure had reached its boiling point. The next thing I know, the deputy and I are in a heated, finger-pointing argument. Thank goodness, my wife was present and chose to stand between us; otherwise, a bad situation may have turned worse.

After a few days and no word from the driver or the authorities, I decided to take matters into my own hands. I called every friend I had in the business and every trucking company I'd ever worked with, pleading with them to keep an eye out for my truck. My wife and I packed a suitcase and headed off for New Jersey. I planned to check every truck stop and rest area along the major routes, realizing that finding my rig was kin to finding a needle in a haystack. I couldn't just sit back and do nothing.

My wife and I spent four days driving and searching when, finally, we caught the break we needed. One of the trucking companies I had reached out to for help, had spotted my truck at a truck stop in New Jersey. Believe it or not, my wife and I were only ten minutes away from where it was parked. Here is the most fantastic part of this story, the truck sat there with keys in the ignition, fuel credit cards all accounted for, and the refrigeration unit running (remember the 44,000 pounds of frozen orange juice.) The trailer seal from the shipper was still intact. The truck appeared neat and orderly, with nothing vandalized or stolen.

Grateful to have my truck back, but faced with how precious time is when hauling frozen orange juice. I filled the reefer up and started back to upstate New York for delivery. I called the broker to give him the good news, who then had to reschedule the delivery to the receiver. As luck would have it, the receiver was being a pain in the ass and wanted me to take the load back to New Jersey to have it checked for contamination. After another day of feuding back and forth on the phone, the receiver finally accepted the frozen orange juice.

Lesson learned I couldn't read drivers as well as I initially thought I could. He never bought us out. He did leave me a lengthy note, detailing how sorry he was that things hadn't worked out between us. I never did find out why he was wanted. I was too happy to have my $100,000 truck back in my possession to even care.

## ~ 12 ~

# NOT LOOKING SO GOOD

If you operate a business long enough and have employees working for you, you're bound to have mishaps. In business for 40 years, I had my share and then some. One particular driver cost me a ton of money. Comically, he was known as Captain.

I had three trucks hauling carrots from Potter, NY, to a processing plant in Salisbury, MD. I was driving the lead truck, followed by Captain, trailed by yet another one of my drivers. Captain was acting a little tired, so we kept talking to him on the CB radio. The plant, our destination, was just two miles ahead, so I felt confident that we could make it that far.

The next noise I hear blaring across the CB radio is my rear driver yelling, "Captain just flipped the truck!" I couldn't believe that in a split second, my Peterbilt and dump trailer could be lying across the middle of the road. If that wasn't bad enough, imagine 25 tons of carrots sprawled across the highway on a scorcher of a day.

The Town's highwaymen came with payloaders in an attempt to clear the road. Only half the load could be salvaged, due in part by using hand shovels. Next, a wrecker was brought to the scene to "upright" the truck and trailer. The State Police were called in and questioned me as to how I was going to get this mess back home. I advised them that a friend of mine was expected soon with his wrecker and that we would be on our way shortly.

The more I thought about this accident, the angrier I got. We'd been so close to our destination, how could this happen? My saving grace, no liquids were leaking from the drivetrain, and it was still holding oil pressure. Looking at the rig, you'd never believe it could run. The sleeper had disconnected during the wreck, its mufflers, and other miscellaneous parts discarded into the dump trailer, which was a sight to be seen, unable to return to its frame, its dump body remained locked in a position two feet in the air.

I turned to Captain and stated, "Get up in that truck and drive it the 400 miles back home!" Everyone thought I was crazy once again. The other driver and I emptied our loads of carrots and loaded up with lime for our return home. While driving down the road, I happened upon a small truck stop. Inside, I questioned whether anyone had spotted my beauty of a truck? A couple of fellas in the diner chuckled, as they recalled seeing Captain slumped over the wheel, taking a nap. With part of the cab missing, he had been awoken by their laughter and subsequent comments concerning his truck's appearance. With scorn, he had fired the wreckage up and headed north. Slumber would have to wait once more.

## ~ 13 ~

# A HITCH IN MY GIDDY-UP

I should have fired Captain after his mishap with the carrots, but past experiences suggested that everyone should get a second chance. Had I listened to my wife, we would have saved a ton of money and been spared some gray hair.

Captain was driving a 2-year-old International, a truck I had originally purchased for myself to drive. This truck was in great shape and condition. One fall afternoon, Captain was driving through Selinsgrove, PA, when the truck immediately ahead of him stopped for a red light. Probably following too closely and unable to stop in time, Captain rear-ends the guy. He called me, advising me of the incident, remaining thankful that no one was injured. As he had barely tagged the other truck, he suggested that a new radiator was all that was needed for him to continue to his destination.

I wanted to take Captain for his word. Time was critical because we were hauling sweet corn in an open trailer, not refrigerated. I contemplated hiring someone to install the radiator right there on the spot, to save a whole lot of time. Fortunately,

I had another driver near Selinsgrove at the time and asked him to stop by for a second opinion. Thank God I did.

The news I heard soon after, confirmed my suspicions. This little fender bender had left my International undrivable, if not totaled. I had the drivers swap the empty trailer headed south with Captains, full of sweet corn. Then summoned a wrecker for my International, it was the last trip the truck would ever have. With the corn delivered, a truck destroyed, it should come with no surprise that Captain and I parted ways. He had become a liability, which I could no longer afford.

## ~ 14 ~

# WRECKERS TO THE RESCUE

My trucks haul a tremendous amount of produce directly from the field. It is customary for us to transport sweet corn, carrots, beans, cabbage, onions, potatoes, cauliflower, beets, and grapes, as well as grains such as field corn, wheat, and soybeans. In the height of the picking season, it would not be uncommon to find my trucks running 24/7. To accomplish such a feat, I hire more drivers on a seasonal basis to get the job done.

Drivers may need to back in and out of strange driveways, never meant for large trucks, often during the middle of the night. When harvesting green beans, my drivers may follow up to 6 harvesters from field to field, covering roughly 6000 acres, which translates to covering a 100-mile radius while trucking some 20,000 tons of green beans. Time is crucial in this process, as the trailers are without refrigeration.

When the phone rings late at night or early in the morning, you can bet it's not a phone call you want. Over the 40 years of trucking produce out of the fields, I can't begin to count how many times I called a wrecker for their assistance. To make matters worse, usually, every mishap would require the help of a second wrecker. The first having the task of pulling the truck forward or backward, while the other would keep the truck and trailer from tipping over. My trailers were loaded to the maximum gross weight of 102,000 pounds, netting anywhere from 32 to 34 tons. Keeping that much weight secure, is by itself complicated. A task made perilous by well-intended drivers, dropping trailer wheels off driveways, and into ditches.

Occasionally, the lean of a full load, in jeopardy of tipping over, would mandate we stall a harvester to have it back alongside a trailer in hopes of saving it until a wrecker could arrive. Other times, we have physically climbed up onto the trailers and unloaded ½ to 2/3rds by hand, to lighten the load.

The bean season usually lasts for about three months. Besides taking care of many acres locally, we regularly traveled to MD, DE, PA, MI, IL, and WI, transporting the beans to the processing plant. During the bean season, I employed two men for the sole purpose of unloading the trucks as they arrived at the plant. These men had the responsibility of running my hydraulic 5th wheel, a device that costs a mere $18,000. It will hoist 50 tons of green beans, without ever cranking a dolly. As easy as it sounds, the first-year operating the 5th wheel was nothing short of a nightmare.

My two "clowns," not to be confused with my father's pair, each made the same mistake, unbelievably with the same trailer. Despite instruction on its safe operation and their steadfast confidence, they both dropped the same trailer on two separate occasions. The first mishap had occurred in the parking lot, the second, directly in front of the plant for everyone to see. Imagine if you will, a trailer which, fully extended, has come free of the 5th wheel, its landing gear lying parallel to the floor. Add in beans which have been obscurely tossed to the left, right and rear, compounded by two wreckers arriving on sight, and you'll have a good idea as to the ensuing chaos which transpired. Thankfully, with additional training and some verbal encouragement, they got the procedure down before the cost of hiring wreckers put me in the hole.

# ~ 15 ~

# A SHADY DEAL

The hauling of green beans was a very profitable venture for our company. They paid enough that I could potentially send a driver 500-600 miles one way, just to pick them up. Typically, I would load my trucks with grain for the trip south, helping to minimize the cost of fuel.

One particular day, I sent two trucks, both loaded with grain, south. Each was to return with green beans from North Carolina. Drivers learn to use the air gauges on the trucks and trailers to estimate the weight of their load. Once full, a driver then proceeds to a certified scale for the actual weight. Imperative that both drivers acquire the bean loads in a timely fashion, I instructed them both to assure their grain loads stay within the legal limit. Well, as you may have guessed, things didn't quite work out that way. One load of grain tipped the scale at 92,000 pounds and the other registered 85,000 pounds. In New York state, my trucks would have been underweight, but in Pennsylvania, 80,000 pounds was the legal limit.

Around midnight our phone rings; a Police Officer from Pennsylvania is on the other end. He informs me that my trucks are too heavy to run through their state. Hoping to get them to the precious beans awaiting them down the road, I begged the officer to let my trucks continue on their way, promising I'd be there by morning's light, to pay the fine. He further advised me that he was impounding both rigs and that each driver would spend the night in jail. Just when I thought my hands were tied, the officer then made the following concession. He stipulated that if I were to bring $3,500 cash immediately, "To cover the fines," he would relinquish the trucks and my drivers. It was music to my ears. My wife and I scooped up what cash we had in the house, and away we went.

I've often pondered that scenario, the officer demanding cash payment rather than a check, needing the money immediately, not the next day. I wondered if my drivers had mentioned that they were en route for some high dollar bean loads. The whole situation just seemed strange and perhaps a little suspicious. Nevertheless, I counted out the hundred dollar bills and my drivers fired up their trucks and continued on their way, following the ass-chewing I gave them for overloading my rigs in the first place.

# ~ 16 ~

# ACCIDENTS WILL HAPPEN

My trucks haul many vegetables during the fall season. We might be carrying a load of green beans or one of sweet corn to the processing plant. In New York state, my trucks are legal to haul 102,000 pounds, gross weight, which makes it impossible for a truck to come to a screeching halt, on-demand.

Regretfully, one of my drivers, with 15 years of experience, whom I consider an excellent driver, was faced with such a dilemma. Northbound, he approached an intersection where east and westbound traffic is required to stop. Regretfully, and without cause, a 90-year-old woman approaching from the east failed to do so. My driver swerved as hard as he could to the left, trying to avoid hitting the vehicle broadside. The car bounced off the right front tire of the truck, causing my Peterbilt and trailer to flip on its side. Emergency crews had their work cut out for them, as they tried to attend to the injured amongst 35 tons of sweet corn scattered across the road.

The 90-year-old woman, in serious condition, was airlifted to Strong Memorial Hospital, in Rochester, NY, where she underwent surgery for neck injuries, thankfully surviving her operation. My driver, shaken to his core, requested a leave of absence, for the balance of the year. Having granted his request, I was delighted to see him back at my truck lot come spring, ready to drive once more.

# ~ 17 ~

# A HISTORICAL MOMENT

During the busy fall season, while looking for new drivers, I interviewed a man in his mid 70's. For the past 30 years, he had owned and operated a grocery store but was seeking a new career experience. He had just passed his CDL test and was anxious to get behind the wheel of a big rig. Call me crazy, but I liked this guy and his work ethic, so I hired him.

Everything was going quite well for my new hire until he found himself lost in Pennsylvania around 2 am. Instead of calling for assistance, he took matters into his own hands. Attempting to turn the tractor and 53' trailer around in a non-designated area, he had backed into a historical stone monument that had stood the test of time for well over 100 years. The commotion awoke a nearby neighbor who bolted out of her house, determined to catch the culprit. This old gal, intent on holding my driver accountable, immediately summoned the Police to the scene. To appease the woman, the Officer issued several tickets and reported the incident to my insurance company.

Several weeks later, my insurance agent and I crossed paths in town. We shook hands and exchanged well-wishes, before continuing on our separate ways. In jest, he hollered back to me, suggesting that, should I find myself in Pennsylvania anytime soon, I stop and see the stone monument I'd replaced for $25,000. Who knew a piece of history could cost so much?

# ~ 18 ~

# CAUGHT ON CAMERA

Usually, my drivers like to leave early in the morning, say 3-4 a.m., which works perfectly, as they arrive at the mills, fully loaded between 7 and 8 a.m. I had my older driver all set for a morning departure with wheat, destined for Pennsylvania. Though I was out of the office that morning, my wife and daughter were available to run the show.

My absence from home was short-lived when I received a phone call, directing me to contact the Pennsylvania State Police. In doing so, a Trooper was quick to inform me that one of my trucks had taken out a utility pole, responsible for transmitting power for an entire village.

My wife called to question the sole driver we had in that area. He inferred that all was well and that he was unaware of anything unusual having occurred. Concluding that there had been a mistake made, my wife called the PA. Trooper back. The officer politely rebutted her disbelief, informing her that they had on film, a truck, with our logo on its side, taking down the pole in question. Sure enough, the law was right. Worse, my driver had lied to my wife (not good.)

Come to find out; this pole had been a pain in the ass for many big rigs. Guidewires, anchoring the high powered pole had been taken down so many times in the past by different trucking companies, that the town had installed a camera to the top of the very pole.

When the truth finally came out, we discovered that my driver had missed his turn and proceeded to turn around at the next available location. As he maneuvered the big rig about, one of the trailer duels had taken the enormous pole to the ground. With neither truck or trailer damaged, he'd been comfortable in letting the incident go unreported. It was the worst mistake he could ever have made. From that moment until the day we retired, my wife never forgave nor trusted him again.

# ~ 19 ~

## WHEN IT RAINS, IT POURS

I ventured outside of my ordinary commodities and took a load that involved harvesting watermelon out of the fields of North Carolina. This trip was supposed to bring a high dollar return for us. Trouble started almost as soon as we arrived. It had begun to rain and never stopped for two days straight. At 8 p.m. on the third day, finally loaded with melons, my rig headed home to Upstate New York. What transpires in the next 8 hours is an owner's worst nightmare.

I was startled awake by the sound of my telephone ringing at 4 a.m. I soon learned that my "melon" truck was involved in an accident in Selinsgrove, PA. I should mention that for this trip we had rented a brand new Volvo. The driver had been traveling on a highway where the four-lane ends before the approaching city limits. The driver, failing to heed traffic signs directing he bare right, had put the truck and trailer on top of the guardrails. The melon's, undeterred by the calamity, remained on board. The truck and trailer, though upright, sat awkwardly perched atop the guardrail. The next phone call I received was from the Department of Environmental Protection. They informed me that I was facing an even bigger problem. One of the fuel tanks had ruptured and was spewing diesel fuel on the ground. Did I neglect to mention we were near the Susquehanna River? When I asked for an estimate on the cost of cleaning up a fuel spill, I almost dropped the phone, $10,000-$15,000 for every 100 gallons of displaced fuel. I quickly fired up another truck and was heading for Pennsylvania to assess the damage and deliver the precious load of watermelons.

Arriving on the scene, I immediately assessed that the trailer would need eight new tires before I considered taking the melons anywhere. Once the tires were mounted, I headed north for delivery. I was grateful for the payment of this load since I happened to notice watermelon juice dripping from the trailer as I pulled away.

For the next several months, the bills kept pouring in. The cost of the rented truck repair was a mere $80,000. The two wreckers that towed the truck and trailer just 10 miles down the road was $15,000. The cost of the eight new tires, plus repairs to the trailer amounted to $7,500. The rented truck was out of commission for six months due to the repairs it needed, and therefore I was billed $15,000 for missed rental revenue. The estimate regarding the spill's cleanup hadn't even been close, adding another $55,000 to my ever-growing debt. In total, this singular event cost me over $172,500 or so I thought.

A year or so later, having licked my wounds clean of the "melon-caper," I received a call from someone within some bureau of Pennysylvania's government. They informed me that I owed $15,000 to the PA Department of Environmental Protection, stemming from the accident. I was to remit payment within thirty days, or my trucks would no longer be allowed to enter or pass through PA. The news was devastating, as over sixty-five percent of my business involved transport within or through Pennsy. I immediately dialed up my insurance agent to see if my policy would cover the bill. It did, but in doing so, my business was venturing into a "high-risk" category. When everything was said and done, the total for this one accident, transitioned to $187,500. To this day, I can't look at a watermelon without feeling some resentment!

## ~ 20 ~

# WHAT DRIVERS WILL DO

When the boss is away, the drivers will play! I contracted to haul carrots harvested on the muck, a low-land valley noted for its fertile, dark soil. The processing plant was 75 miles away. One of my drivers and a competitor of mine were racing with loaded trucks to see who could reach the plant first. My guy was in the lead as he entered the front gate. Traveling way too fast as he approached the entrance to the plant, he laid both my truck and trailer on its side. 35 ton of carrots were spread across the front lawn of the plant, what a picture. I quickly hired some help to pick up the carrots. Next came purchasing speedy-dry for the hydraulic oil and diesel which had spilled. Grateful that no one had called the D.E.C., now in a high-risk category with my insurance carrier, I decided that the cost of the wrecker needed to upright the truck and trailer was something I would pay myself. Unamused by the driver's behavior and avoidable expenses, I fired him.

Another accident, which occurred in New York City, may have been thwarted had common sense prevailed. When a sign denotes a bridge's height as 12' and your truck and trailer stand at 13'6", isn't it obvious that you won't fit? My driver contested that we had gone under that bridge in the past. Alerted by the sudden jolt to his neck, realizing his error in judgment, he began to back up, hoping to free himself of the bridge. In doing so, the reefer unit, attached to the front of the trailer was pulled free, left to lay against the sleeper of a new Peterbilt. In an attempt to make things right, he'd borrowed a chain, ratcheting the reefer unit back to the trailer to continue his journey home. We ended up making a dry box van out of the refrigerated trailer, ending its ability to be utilized for hauling produce after that.

I will never forget the phone call I received from one of my drivers telling me that he had a slight problem. There appeared to be a small hole in the roof of his trailer. He then proceeded to explain that he had "touched" a bridge before his last delivery, and while there had been no damage to the product, duct tape would fix the hole temporarily. Can you feel my hesitation? His quick thinking would have him in Hershey, PA., picking up a reefer load of chocolate without so much as a sigh.

Within fifteen minutes, I received a call from a very perplexed shipper, wondering if I had seen my trailer lately? I confessed that while I hadn't, I understood that it had a small hole, easily repaired with duct tape. The shipper then screamed, "Small hole?" It appeared that half of the trailer's roof was missing, "It's been opened like a can of sardines." The trailer subsequently arrived home empty, needing over twelve feet of its roof replaced. The City of Hershey, Pennsylvania, wouldn't have had enough duct tape to mend that hole!

# ~ 21 ~

# THOSE WERE THE DAYS

I have had many good times along the way, and some funny stories happened as well. One such story involved a driver in Ohio, loaded with sweet corn destined for Bergen, N.Y. This corn, picked by a machine and dumped into an open-top trailer, was headed for a canning factory. My driver, playing it smart, avoided the toll roads because his load was too heavy. It seems the State Police, equally intelligent, had portable scales set up on back roads as well. My truck, overweight by 3,000 pounds, was halted until the load was of legal weight.

My driver thought I had lost my mind when I told him what to do next. I told him to walk into a nearby McDonald's and ask to speak with the Manager. Explaining that his truck was not allowed to proceed down the road until it was of legal weight. We were hoping that we could sell some sweet corn in his parking lot, which would lighten the load. Believe it or not, the manager agreed to my scheme. Our second obstacle was convincing the State Trooper to allow us to move the truck some 500 feet into the McDonald's parking lot. It must have been our lucky day because even he went for this crazy plan.

The driver released the tailgate on his trailer and gently let some corn fall to the blacktop. Word spread like wildfire. Sweet corn was being sold by the dozens, to local folks whose cars lined the road. Everyone was eager to purchase some delicious sweet corn well below market prices. It only took a couple of hours to sell the 3,000 pounds necessary to be of legal weight. The Manager at McDonald's received compensation for his hospitality, and everyone was happy. My driver continued on his merry way with just a $350.00 overweight ticket. Tales of our adventure carried across three states. Truckers from Ohio, Pennsylvania, and New York were all talking about the awesome sweet corn sale at McDonald's on their CB radios. The processing plant even called my office to comment on this little venture. Losing 3,000 pounds of corn sounded better than losing the whole load (50,000 pounds) in the hot sun.

It was quite the sight when my driver walked into my office carrying McDonald's bags full of cash. He'd sold enough corn that day to pay for the overweight ticket, then split the balance with me.

## ~ 22 ~

# GETTING YOUR ATTENTION

Hauling sweet corn out of Maryland was commonplace for my drivers. One afternoon, as three of my trucks, approached a bridge in Maryland, they spotted a DOT checkpoint up ahead. Anxious, the first driver, realizing his seatbelt wasn't fastened, grabbed for his belt in a panic. In his efforts to avoid being issued a ticket, he'd accidentally engaged the pto switch utilized for raising the dump trailer into the air. The checkpoint, a drive-by, didn't mandate that all trucks pull in. As he hadn't been directed to step free from the truck's cab, he never had the chance to notice his mistake until impact. My aluminum trailer struck a steel brace on the bridge like a bullseye. The collision caved its front end, rearward by 2 feet, leaving the roll tarp dangling in the breeze. Jolted by his negligence, the driver backed up, permitting the lift to lower the trailer to its proper resting position.

Once on the bridge, there was no turning back. The driver continued to the other side, some four miles in length, where he and the other drivers met up. Together, they conspired what should become of the 40' tarp, now stretched upon the highway. With adrenaline flowing through their veins, the DOT boys, a short piece behind, they diligently strapped the tarp to the side of the trailer and hauled ass out of town before they could be issued any tickets. One of the drivers suggested that the trailer striking the bridge sounded like a bomb exploding.

When they finally arrived at the cornfield, they questioned whether or not to load the damaged trailer. They consulted with me, and I determined that they could. Delivery of the sweet corn went without further delay, albeit in a thirty-eight-foot trailer rather than a forty. I shudder to imagine the outcome, had the trailer been any higher in the air. The price of repairing the bridge would likely have been in the millions. I accepted my check for less money because of the smaller trailer size, knowing how much money I could have lost. I repaired the trailer and walked away, considering myself lucky that day. My insurance company felt the same way.

# ~ 23 ~

# WHAT'S THAT SMELL?

One morning I answered a call from a State Police Officer in Pennsylvania. He informed me that he had detained one of my drivers and truck at a DOT checkpoint, near the Town of Towanda. He further advised that on approach to the driver's side of the cab, he'd noted a peculiar aroma aloft in the air.

As the story unfolds, I learn that my driver of twenty years was driving my $100,000 rig down the road, stoned! In desperation, he had attempted to hide his marijuana pipe between the seats; to his surprise, when looking left, he's facing the Officer standing on the running board of my truck. I knew immediately that my driver was in serious trouble. The PA. State Police wasted no time hauling him to jail.

The Officer I had spoken with, was uncertain as to what policy dictated would occur next, confessing that his trooper barracks had never experienced anything like this before. Ultimately, they chose to have blood drawn in an attempt to confirm the content of the pipe. After many hours and numerous phone calls back and forth, they decided that, while my driver couldn't drive a DOT vehicle, like the tractor and trailer, he would be permitted to operate a car. Should I make the 100-mile journey ASAP, I would save my truck and trailer from being impounded.

I drove my car down to the troopers' barracks, not knowing what awaited me. Fortunately, my driver was released, receiving a ticket for possession of a controlled substance. He was allowed to drive my car back home.

How different the outcome would have been, had it happened today? Following the Court prescribed class-time, perhaps some blood tests, my driver garnered the right to get behind the wheel once again.

## ~ 24 ~

# POOR FUEL MILEAGE

I once hired a female driver. Everything was great in the beginning. Her interview had gone well, and her resume had checked out. She certainly knew how to handle a truck. She started driving one fall during our busy time, hauling squash and cauliflower to New York City. It worked out perfectly, as she loved going to the city, while most of my other drivers dreaded those trips. The loads paid substantially, and she made a percentage off the load. Her take-home, at week's end, was considerable. I had no issues with her performance. She was completing three round trips a week, from Stanley, NY to New York City.

I've learned over my 40 years in the trucking business that when things are going too good to be true, you best tread carefully, as it's often when the shit hits the fan.

Almost predictably, she begins making two rounds per week rather than three. Excuses ensue as to why she's stopped answering her phone, while I'm running interference with growers, upset by missed loading and unloading appointments.

Worse, she had stopped reporting to me on her locations and delivery times.

My wife, a consummate companion in our home office, had long retained records of fuel intake on each truck. Drivers were responsible for all fueling, while on the road. Subsequently, our monthly fuel statements were sizable. One morning, over coffee, an adding machine nearby, she brought to my attention that our once stellar employee was averaging only two miles per gallon of diesel. How could that be possible? What had I missed?

I approached my "Shirley Muldowney," sure that even a lead foot couldn't account for such fuel consumption. It wasn't until I suggested involving law enforcement that she confessed her whole story. With tears rolling down her cheeks, she admitted to two criminal offenses. It seems her father, who also owned a big rig, was hauling grapes to New York City at the same time she was hauling produce for me. They would meet at a truck stop and fuel his truck up using my credit card, thus explaining why her rig appeared to have such shitty fuel mileage.

Next, she confessed why she didn't answer her phone and could only make two trips a week. She would haul a load of grapes for her father with my truck and then pocket the earnings. She had brass for sure. Blind-sided, I abruptly ended her employment, grateful to have the truth.

## ~ 25 ~

# MY WIFE THE LAWYER

I dedicate the following chapter to my wife, though she deserves much more than words can express. Her clear thinking has withstood many a sleepless night. Her composure, undeterred by the countless scenarios which have, throughout the years, jeopardized our livelihood. The following is but one of many examples.

A driver was hauling produce to a processing plant in Pittsburgh, PA., built over 100 years ago. Back then, a day cab and 40' trailer were considered huge, a rig exceeding 70' in length, unimaginable.

All of my drivers complained about backing into such a narrow space to unload. The challenge involved backing into an unlit area marked off only by paint and curbing that lined one side of the platform.

My driver pulled into this plant for a 1:00 am delivery, and by 2:00 am, my phone was ringing off the hook. As the driver was backing up to the dock, the receiver directed him to pull forward, attempting to square the trailer with the dock. When the truck pulled ahead, the top of the opened trailer door caught upon some air duct that is responsible for cooling the entire plant. On the ground lay numerous hinges, my trailer door, and ductwork ripped from the ceiling of this plant. Hysteria had ensued.

I instructed my driver to take all the pictures he could of the damages then forward them to me. The next call I received was from the plant manager, placing all the blame on an inexperienced driver while informing me of pending expenses. The plant would have to close, and without refrigeration, products would have to be shipped elsewhere, yadda, yadda, yadda. I hung up on him, only to have the head of the canning company call, asking about my insurance coverage. Emails started flying between the factory, my insurance company, and myself, as estimates for repair continued to grow.

The correspondence between the three of us went on for at least six months. The canning factory kept adding to the repair bill that my insurance company was required to pay. When the total reached $50,000, my wife and I made a trip to the canning factory, to see the damage for ourselves. All of the pictures from the incident made it hard to visualize blame being my drivers.

We were greeted at the plant by a committee of six associates. They had one of their trailers backed into place, at the dock for representation. It was my first time at this plant, and I soon realized why my drivers despised coming here to unload. The plant had made no accommodations for either the length or the width of trailers since constructed. Though work was underway to replace the ductwork, to my amazement, they were reinstalling it, exactly where it had been previously.

Thank goodness my wife had come along, my temper blinded my ability to see what should have been evident to everyone. She first asked whether the trailer currently parked at the dock was 96 inches wide, or 102". Before anyone could respond, she deduced that while both units shared identical wheelbases, allowing both the ability to back up to the dock, the physical characteristics of the containers themselves were off by 6 inches. Amidst hushed conversation and a fair share of head nodding, the blame had transferred to the plant. The old dock and nearby ductwork could no longer receive loads from modern-day equipment, mine, or anyone else's.

We showed ourselves out of the facility that day, feeling pretty good. The emails soon stopped, and my insurance company sighed a relief, knowing we had won the battle. I treated my new found attorney to a great dinner on our way home. I even gave her a raise in salary, for having thought things through. We never delivered fresh produce to that canning factory again, its payout didn't warrant the risk.

## ~ 26 ~

# MY YOUNGER DAYS

I was no different from any other young driver thinking he could be "King" of the road. While I've mentioned the high jinks and shortcomings of several drivers, in fairness to them, I had my share as well. When I first started, I was driving full time and dispatching on the go. I trucked lawn and garden fertilizer for Agway from Sunday night through Saturday afternoon. With most loads headed east, I was driving 500-700 miles daily to Massachusetts, Vermont, Connecticut, or Long Island. As electronic log entries weren't mandated yet, it was easy to be creative with paper logs, an occasional duplicate, to skirt the law.

My brother and I were headed for Long Island one winter night, highways were terrible, as it had been snowing and sleeting all week long. I was driving my Peterbilt, with its new motor. We were loading on a Thursday night, destined to deliver the following morning. I knew my trailer brakes were way out of adjustment, which was customary by the end of the week. We rented van trailers and would service their brakes, along with the truck, on weekends. The trucking industry was yet to see automatic brake adjusters. Instead, a driver would lay on their back, among the stones and dirt, to manually adjust them.

We were heading east on route 17, and the snow just kept coming down that night. I was in the lead and ready to descend for three miles down Wilkesboro Mountain. Usually, this decline wasn't a problem, drop two, maybe three gears, and it's smooth sailing, but when you're half asleep and forget to downshift, hold on tight! My brother starts hollering on the CB radio, "Watch out for the snow-covered curves coming up." When I realized my mistake, it was too late to slow down. My brakes were so far out of adjustment that slowing down was out of the question. The brakes continued to get hotter and hotter every time I applied them. A lot went through my mind, uncertain as to how the situation would end. Not only was the speedometer out of numbers, but the tachometer was too. Unable to assist any more than looking away, my brother watched on as smoke billowed from my brakes, the drums were on fire.

The CB radio was alive with truckers, yelling their advice to slow down. I clenched the steering wheel so hard that my fingers grew numb. By God's grace, I was on a four-lane highway, which mitigated hitting someone head-on, but did nothing to slow me down. I traveled down that mountain and up the other side without once touching the throttle.

When my truck finally came to a screeching halt with smoke circling its exterior, I climbed out of the cab and kissed the ground before me. The adrenaline running through my veins when my truck peeked 100 mph, was overwhelming. What held my new Detroit engine together, I will never know, but I am sure glad it did. When my brother got done chewing my ass for such a stupid move, we proceeded to adjust my brakes right there along the shoulder of the road. Lying on the cold, wet pavement never felt so good.

Today's strict enforcement of rules and safety regulations, self-adjusting brakes, and the use of jake brakes (engine braking), help to ensure the welfare of truck drivers everywhere. My Pete had neither, I have but the good Lord to thank for my safety that day.

## ~ 27 ~

# INVINCIBLE

Young and naive, the world was mine to conquer. My biggest downfall growing up may well have been my inability to say no, especially if money was involved, a trait I likely acquired from my father.

A local farmer once offered me the chance to haul his cucumbers to Paterson, NJ., I grabbed the opportunity without hesitation, knowing the return would be substantial. I should have realized that a daily run of 600 miles was enough to endure, but I didn't. Instead, I found myself also hauling wheat locally. This pace was daunting, and by my fifth day, with little if any sleep, my ass was dragging. In passing, I ran into an old trucking buddy. We conversed for a couple of minutes, and, with my exhaustion apparent, he offered me a "stay awake" remedy, concerned that I remain alert while driving.

With more and more work coming my way, I decided to try my buddies "little white pills." I remember crossing the Pocono Mountains on Route 380 one night when my sleepy eyes snapped wide open. The whole left side of my body went numb. I pulled off on the shoulder of the road and called my wife to tell her my location. I thought my time had come, and I wanted to say goodbye, insisting that I would love her forever. She had a hard time understanding my slurred speech but knew I was in trouble. I thought my heart was going to explode.

I thought help had arrived when I spotted a State Trooper pulling off the road. Unfortunately, he had interpreted my hand wave as a sign that no help was needed. Time crawled by as I sat on the shoulder of the road. My pleas for assistance on the CB radio went unanswered. I knew there was a rest area at the base of the hill on Route 80; perhaps someone there would come to my aid. With my heart racing, crippled by anxiety, I drove my rig on the shoulder of the highway for the next five miles.

I finally reached the rest area, only to find a single truck in the parking lot. Not knowing what else to do, I awoke the sleeping driver and begged for his help. With his assistance, I walked to the restroom and splashed cold water on my face hoping that it would help matters. As we exited the building, I collapsed to the ground. My legs were numb and were unable to support my weight. I was in a heap of trouble.

Realizing how serious my condition was, the trucker then placed a call to 911, staying beside me until the ambulance arrived. The EMTs quickly checked my vitals, but everything appeared to be within an acceptable range. They ruled out a stroke and heart attack but stipulated I would need further testing to confirm a diagnosis. Feeling somewhat relieved, I convinced the crew to let me drive another 75 miles to my destination.

I traveled the remaining distance, with flashers on, going about 40 m.p.h. to reach the processing plant. I continuously had to pull off the road and gain my composure. The fear of another attack loomed over me. I called the receiver at the plant, explaining the load would be a few hours late, eventually arriving at noon, rather than the scheduled 5 am. While there, I attempted to catch some sleep. My body, still wired from the pills, resisted.

The drive home was the longest in my career. With panic as close as the passenger's seat, I would pull off numerous times, anxious that another attack was threatening, before making it to our driveway. I fought similar feelings on and off countless years after that, especially while driving at night. I had learned my lesson, never again would I substitute a sound sleep with the promise found in a pill.

## ~ 28 ~

## COMPROMISE

A friend and employee of 27 years had started his career as a truck driver, hauling produce from Florida to New York. A typical run would involve loading assorted fruits and vegetables at five or better warehouses while making his way north through the state. Occasionally, some produce would need to be hand loaded, then separated on the trailer, depending upon where in New York it was to be delivered. A tedious task on the best of days. Once full, he traveled the balance of 1500 miles, all in less than 30 hours, with very little sleep. The horror stories I heard him tell, reliving circumstances beyond his control, while exhausted and behind the wheel, reflect many of my own.

Despite having spent much of the day loading, indifferent to the miles before him, receivers would demand delivery within a 24-hour window. Exhausted, all hell broke loose one afternoon, when my buddy arrived late with a load. Sleep-deprived, he had pulled into a rest area for a brief spell to catch a nap. When he arrived two hours late, the receiver was in no mood for any excuses or apologies. A flurry of shouting commenced, and the ill-tempered receiver soon learned not to poke the proverbial bear.

Out-gunned, so to speak, the receiver, with equal portions of profanity, was asked if he'd prefer to pick up his product alongside the road by himself because a rollover had occurred. He further advised, "Harold that if he were in that big of a hurry for his ......cherry tomatoes, they'd be back at the trucking terminal 50 miles south and he could damn well get them himself."

Harold wasn't quite so cocky when "Big Dick" finished with him. Instead, he seemed to grow a sense of appreciation, eventually becoming good friends with each other.

I respectfully offer my gratitude to this driver, for his twenty-seven years of service and devotion to my business. In his forty years of driving, he'd covered over four million miles, never having caused an accident due to lack of sleep. He warrants my praise.

~ 29 ~

# THE DRAG RACE

I should have been suspicious when a manager at the CAT repair shop questioned who had been messing with my motor; instead, I pleaded ignorance. The only reason my Pete was in that shop, and not at my local mechanic, was for recall work. The manager was perplexed as to how one of my Peterbilts could be diagnostically showing over 600 horsepower. He informed me that my motor would not withstand the stress and suggested that I return it to factory default. When I conveyed his news to my mechanic, he only laughed. Nicknamed, "The Doctor," he was a surgeon on CAT motors. This guy could perform miracles on an old CAT engine, absent all the new electronics.

One afternoon, an opportunity arose to drive one of my trucks, Doc, had modified. I was to deliver a 22-ton load, 25 miles down the road. After traveling five miles or so, I began to wonder if I had hooked up to the wrong dump trailer? There was no way one fully loaded could be pulling with such ease. Confident that I had, I physically climbed up its side to see for myself, shocked to see a fully loaded trailer above my wheels. When I returned, I asked Doc how my truck, carrying 22 tons, could drive and handle like a car going down the road?

The story which unfolded next explained the puzzlement from the CAT manager. Four of my drivers, including Doc's brother, were well-established drinking buddies. Whenever their trucks needed servicing, they would complain that they needed more horsepower to run smoothly and efficiently, and Doc came to the rescue. Their scheme helped to explain my increased fuel consumption per mile. I wasn't too upset with the boys, as we hauled heavier loads for a short distance compared to those distances traveled by big freight companies. My only regret came from being left out of the loop.

With a full understanding of the magic conjured beneath the hood of my trucks, I had to see more. Owning a pair of International's the same year, equipped with the same motor, their only difference was in their transmissions. One had a 13 speed and the other a 15. One day, when Doc's brother and I were beside each other, each carrying 30 tons of wheat, we got the brilliant idea to race. We left Doc's shop in Geneva, NY, and traveled 10 miles to my trucking lot. We were neck and neck as we moved down a four-lane highway, but I was soon inhaling his exhaust. Doc's brother won the race, though I suspect his engine may have been under Doc's stethoscope longer than mine. The adage about blood being thicker than water had proven right.

Within months, reality set in. My little drag race proved to be costly. My transmission had gone out, while Doc's brother lost both rear-drives. My moment of fun had cost me $10,000. Whenever Doc and I would reminisce about the race, a peculiar smile would appear on his face. I never knew if it was from guilt or pleasure.

As time went by, I drove less, working more from the office. I missed the long trips and seeing fellow truckers, the unforgettable sights one sees on the road. I still take an occasional run with a truck, if only to the repair shop. Once in your blood, it becomes a part of you.

# ~ 30 ~

# BUYING MORE TRUCKS

The rising cost of new Peterbilts, enslaved with fuel emissions equipment, made it tough to turn a profit. With that said, we quickly took to purchasing used Petes to keep replacements beneath $100,000. In 2005 I bought a 2003 long nose Pete with a CAT 6NZ engine. It came with all the bells and whistles, including a price tag of $3000 over budget. It seemed like one of my best investments. It ran perfectly and was seldom in the shop for any repairs, up until it was involved in a rollover that is.

Destroyed, we salvaged the engine, transmission, and rear ends' from the wreckage. Call me crazy, many have, but I decided to resurrect the truck as best I might, purchasing a glider kit directly from Peterbilt. A 2015 long nose absent an engine and tranny. I found a shop in Turbotville, PA., able to retrofit my former truck components into the new Pete's shell. Many parts of which were interchangeable, despite the difference in years, courtesy of Peterbilt engineering.

The end justified the means. After spending $100,000 on the cab and chassis, another $25,000 on mechanics, I had a great truck able to avoid the fuel emission standards imposed on the new ones.

Still looking to increase my fleet size, in 2008, I purchased another used Peterbilt with a CAT twin-turbo engine. At $105,000, truck #14 remained a better solution than dealing with the fuel emission problems associated with the new motors. It traveled up and down the highway with nothing more than routine maintenance until its odometer read 700,000 miles when the big CAT earned its first overhaul.

What came next was both unnecessary and shameful. Just 15,000 miles beyond her overhaul, the truck had blown a radiator hose. The driver, anxious to get home, continued on his way, without topping off the CATS reservoir. He had arrived back at the yard, swapped out the blown hose with a new one, then topped off the radiator with antifreeze, washing his hands of the incident.

I stopped by my shop, located adjacent to the truck yard, observing #14 parked in front of the overhead door. On approach, I noted ten empty gallon jugs of antifreeze in the trash barrel; my curiosity surfaced. I climbed up into the cab of the truck, hoping to find everything satisfactory. To my surprise, she wouldn't even turn over. Overheated upon arrival, the engine, absent any fluids, had set up!

To suggest that I was upset would be a vast understatement. The driver's maneuver never brought to my attention, may well have gone undetected, had I not happened along. My blood pressure peaked, I brought my driver in for a meeting; it was the last we would ever share. Amidst the conversation, void common sense, his stunt would now require me to hire a wrecker to haul the truck to a repair shop, where I would spend another $20,000 to overhaul the engine yet again. I swear drivers can make or break a trucking company.

In 2010, I still avoided emission problems by acquiring used trucks. Scarcity was becoming a problem. With prices on the rise, I was lucky to find a 2006 long nose Pete, also equipped with a twin-turbo CAT, for $106,000. Trucking rates weren't climbing as fast as the price tags were on new rigs. Unaffordable, everyone sought used ones, further elevating costs.

With business growing, so did my fleet. When a local freight company went belly-up, an opportunity presented itself. Over 400 big International tractors with sleepers were up for auction. Forever in love with Peterbilts, I was unable to ignore a good deal when I saw one, I purchased two trucks. Both were 2006 models with 350k miles on them, costing $27,000 each. Packaged with ISX Cummings power plants, I felt confident in my purchase. The trucks were well maintained, and their emissions were limited to EGR valves only. With an International dealer less than ten miles away, both rigs were good money makers for us. Despite their proven durability, it's challenging to find a driver who has ever driven a Pete, willing to drive an International. With that said, contradicting myself to some extent, the worst lemon I ever purchased was, in fact, a Peterbilt.

One day while in Utica, NY, I stopped at my favorite Pete dealership. Though my favorite salesman had retired, I was dealing with one of the owners directly, so I still felt reassured. A truck had just come into the dealership on trade, its engine overhauled. I could purchase it for $108,000, with warranty remaining on the engine. It was music to my ears, or so I thought.

In hindsight, I wish I had done my research, as both '07 and '08's with ISX Cummins engines came equipped with "trash-can" filters and exhaust gas recovery valves, known for significant issues directly attributed to emissions. My 2008 Peterbilt had traveled a mere 5,000 miles when news came from my driver that the motor had blown. I couldn't believe it and neither could the dealership. A wrecker retrieved my Pete, returning it to Utica for repairs. The dealership absorbed the price of replacing the block and head on the motor, a pricey undertaking for sure. The truck was out of commission for thirty days and at one of our busiest times of the year, but I remained optimistic, grateful the bill wouldn't be mine this time around.

I should have sold the truck right then, as nightmares continued to follow. This truck spent more time in the shop for repairs then it did traveling down the highway. None of my drivers wanted a thing to do with it, fearing they'd find themselves broken down alongside the road. In an attempt to break even on our investment, we deregulated the emissions on the motor, hoping the truck could then spend more time on the highway. Though costly, it did improve the performance of the unit. It was never a moneymaker, but I walked away rich in knowledge, having learned the value of homework ahead of significant purchases.

I had a tough time convincing my wife that we should purchase another truck, following the disaster with the 2008 Pete. Nonetheless, we'd enjoyed a couple of outstanding years in the trucking business, and it was time to pay Uncle Sam. I planned on buying another glider kit from the Peterbilt dealership, hoping to have it show on our taxes as a deduction, but I had failed to consider that having it delivered in November, would not give enough time for the truck to be licensed and on the road before year-end. I was in a pickle. Our accountant, who refused to work in gray areas, suggested we either reinvest in our business or pay-up. Out on the limb, I learned that a Peterbilt dealership in Rochester, NY, had just what I needed. A brand new, black cherry, 2014 high bunk Pete, with a 550 ISX Cummins engine, waiting to be sold. This new truck would be the write off we needed now, while the glider kit would work for the following year, problem solved. My wife took several deep breaths as we discussed our options, as I saw them. She wasn't thrilled about going further into debt but ultimately concurred with me.

She was right to be reluctant, the days of spending $100,000 as my top dollar for a new truck were long gone. The 2014 Pete, combined with the purchase of either a dump or tank trailer, I can't recall which, totaled $235,000. It makes me feel old knowing that my first truck and dump trailer together cost $35,000. Representing a 571% increase on the expense side of the business, I wish the income side of the scale had balanced equally.

Trucks with fuel emissions and liquid diesel exhaust fluid are mandated by the government nowadays. New engines just can't perform as the old ones had, restricted to comply with regulations set by the DOT. My personal favorite is the 6NZ CAT engine, I had six in my fleet, and each had over a million miles beneath them.

# ~ 31 ~

# A LUCKY DAY

Trucking is in my blood, and whenever I got the opportunity to help my drivers out, I would jump at the chance. I frequently would hook and unhook particular trucks and trailers for the boys, making their job easier come the next day. I never encouraged drivers to switch trailers in the dark if it was avoidable. The winter months were always the worst for problems developing at the truck lot. You never knew if the truck or trailer might be stuck or frozen in the snow, which had accumulated overnight, so I was always available to lend a helping hand.

One afternoon I hooked one of my Peterbilts to a 53' van trailer for a driver to save him the trouble of accomplishing the task at midnight. I paired the two together, as usual, setting the trailer brakes and trying to pull them apart by easing out on the clutch. I also climbed out of the truck and visually inspected the pin. With everything hooked up correctly, he was ready for the trip ahead.

My driver pulled out of my truck lot around 12:30 am, and by 1:00 am, my phone was ringing loudly. He had driven just twelve miles down the road with the loaded trailer when it had come unhooked from the 5th wheel. Since his departure, he had stopped at six separate intersections, while turning either left or right, three times. When pulling forward from a stoplight, the trailer had gracefully detached, coming to rest in the middle of an intersection. My driver was furious, profanely pointing the finger at me, confident that the mishap had been my fault, having hooked the trailer to the truck improperly.

I quickly fired up another truck, and away I went to the rescue. I arrived on the scene to find Deputies directing traffic around the trailer, fortunate to have had it happen, in a small farm town, in the early morning hours. I backed up to the trailer and was surprised to find the landing gear was still in working order, considering the jolt it must have endured. The trailer survived the drop, due in part to a small load and the slow momentum applied when taking off from the light. With a lot of sweat and cranking on the dollies, we connected the trailer to the truck I had brought and headed home without a ticket issued.

I couldn't figure out what had gone wrong. Usually, if a trailer is not attached correctly, it will come off the 5th wheel within a few feet, especially if it's loaded. I didn't understand how it had gone 12 miles with all the stopping and turning involved before it decided to unhook. All these questions, plus others, raced through my mind as I drove the trailer back home. I had been lucky this time around and needed answers to prevent it from happening again.

I took the truck to my buddy's shop, hoping that he could shed some light on what had gone wrong. It was to his amazement and mine when we discovered that the 5th wheel attached to my tractor was obsolete. I had bought the used truck, unaware that the previous owner had installed a single latch 5th wheel, no longer of legal use, for what should be apparent. When the latch broke, the trailer would unhook without warning, who knew?

I felt better knowing the cause of the trouble, reassured that I hadn't done anything wrong. I am also grateful that the trucking industry now requires a double latch system on all of its 5th wheels. Over the years, I have experienced many scary situations, some avoidable, others not. My driver, uninjured, lived to drive another day. We had been lucky. Could you imagine that trailer coming unhooked at sixty-five mph, much less crossing into oncoming traffic, at night? It still gives me shivers.

## ~ 32 ~

# THE MISSING LOAD

Occasionally, during our busy times of the year, we would contract some of our work out to better service our customers. Some of these owner-operators would pull their trailers, other times mine, whichever worked out best for the job. My neighbor, one such operator, had worked with me for many years. He usually hauled fuel for a company in Western New York, but when business was slow, he'd hook up to my liquid fertilizer tanker, and away he went. My business boomed in the spring, hauling fertilizer to local farmers mandated we hire extra help.

My trucks were running nonstop, with back to back loads, so I sought out my neighbor for some help on a load headed north. I called the farmer for directions since none of my drivers were familiar with this customer. My neighbor obliged.

I was dumbfounded when I received a call from the farmer wanting to know where his fertilizer was? I proceeded to tell him that his shipment had arrived three days earlier. I didn't know what to say when he informed me that he was staring at his empty fertilizer tank that very moment. I tried to remain calm, promising that I would call him right back. How does a tanker full of fertilizer just disappear?

The story that unfolded was nothing short of a nightmare. The dairy farmer had located the bill for his fertilizer in the cab of a tractor on his property. He also discovered that the fertilizer had gone into the wrong tank, the herd had been drinking liquid fertilizer instead of whey for three days. Whey is routinely used in liquid supplements for dairy cows and very beneficial to calves as an energy supplement. The farmer was enraged. He demanded that another load of fertilizer, costing $15,000 be delivered to his farm immediately so that he could plant his corn on schedule. On the second trip north, I dispatched one of my drivers with the fertilizer and asked that he scope out the surroundings. As luck would have it, the whey and fertilizer tank are only 10' apart, and no labels were present, distinguishing one tank from the other. A couple of months went by with no further word from the farmer, but I knew it was too good to be true. The phone calls and meetings soon began to pour in. A fight was developing on all sides.

The farmer refused to pay for either load of fertilizer and felt justified in suing for damages. The milk production on his farm was below average, and newborn calves were mysteriously dying. The list goes on and on. He planned to sue me, the owner of the truck, and the company that sold him the fertilizer. We all agreed to meet with the farmer in hopes of settling this matter out of court. Making matters worse, the hired hand who had directed the driver to the wrong tank, denied doing so. The meeting soon turned into finger-pointing, with little proof to back up either story. I left, sure I would be part of a massive lawsuit, where hundreds of thousands of dollars were at stake, but whose?

I quickly contacted my insurance agent and told him to prepare for the worst. We held our breath as days turned into weeks without a word of any legal action coming our way. Finally, my agent received the news we had long-awaited. The farmer was unable to provide enough evidence to support his claim. As blame was undeterminable, my neighbor and I were off the hook. While I never learned who paid for the fertilizer, my insurance agent was glad to see the case closed. Luck had befriended us once again.

# ~ 33 ~

# GOING OUT ON TOP

At 64 years old, I was making deals and seeing my business thrive, but for how long could I persevere? My oldest daughter had worked in my office for all of ten years, my sister for five. Neither had an interest in taking over the operation, having witnessed the headaches that arose after 5 pm. The phone calls from drivers with flat tires, breakdowns, missed appointments, rejected loads, the unforeseen accidents.

My youngest daughter had become an established school teacher within the district, and my only son had found success in the banking industry. He had learned early in life that a trucking business meant hard work and long hours. I wasn't surprised when he shied away; he'd greased trucks and trailers as a young teenager, a process that often consumed most weekends, regardless of the weather. My shop was too small for the trucks to pull into, so the greasing happened outside, all year long. When he announced that he was hanging up his grease gun, he wasn't kidding. Surprised that he was ready to throw in the towel after only a couple of years, he laughed, "It's been nine years Dad, not two."

With timing crucial, I debated whether to sell out now, when my business was thriving or keep going to reap our well-earned profits? My company was both stable and reliable. I never had to take on any new clients. Though the commodities we hauled might change from season to season, the contacts I had developed over forty years, remained consistent. It was a good feeling knowing that I had established that type of rapport in the trucking industry.

It was my son, the banker, who helped me decide to sell. We were talking one day when out of the blue, he asked me if I would consider selling the business, if he was able to find a buyer. Having given the idea very little thought, much less retirement, I deferred answering his question until first speaking with his mother.

My wife and I pondered our son's question at length, there were both pros and cons to consider. Ultimately, we decided that if the right requirements were met, we would give an offer, our consideration, letting our son know the same. He, in turn, approached one of his current clients, discussing a possible buy-out. After several meetings, and ongoing dialogue, in six months' time, an agreement had been forged. The buyers were more than fair in meeting my requests.

The transaction involved buying most of my equipment while hiring all my drivers at the same wages and benefits they were making with me. I sold them ten Peterbilts and 35 trailers in the deal, leaving two Internationals and a few trailers, available for local purchase. My brother was also hired by the new owners. I transferred all client and contact information as well.

June 15th, 2018, a local trucking company took possession of my equipment. My drivers would keep working with their trucks and haul for the same customers, but their wages would come from a new source. They had been loyal to me, some for twenty years, I wanted what was best for them. They'd earned my respect.

## ~ 34 ~

# LETTING GO

The first few weeks after selling out were difficult to manage. Our closing agreement stipulated that I would work for the new owners for three weeks helping to train their staff and put together deals, knowing I wouldn't see the benefits. Furthermore, I couldn't be part of any trucking business for at least ten years, allowing their new business to flourish.

It was tough seeing my trucks on the road with a different name painted on their doors. I spent many sleepless nights wondering if I had made the right decision. It was hard letting go of a business that my wife and I had built together for over 40 years. I never anticipated missing the ring of phones, but I did. I'd catch myself checking my cell phone countless times a day to see if it was working. Once on call 24/7, I soon found the silence overwhelming.

My youngest daughter, observing my exhaustion following a busy day at the office, once requested, I give her my cell phone. She asked that I guess how many calls I had either received or sent that day. My guess of 100 fell short by 99. Imagine the actual number had she reviewed the call log from the two phone lines in the office.

I miss everything, my old customers, my connections, watching the money coming in, a life with purpose. I have been out of the trucking business for almost two years now, and the new owners still employ all my old drivers, servicing my same accounts. The selling of my business was one of the smoothest and easiest deals I was ever part of.

## ~ 35 ~

# FULL CIRCLE

Selling the trucking business left my wife and I, for the first time in our lives, with very little debt, we were in new territory. We consulted with our accountant, who offered us several options. Diversified, I purchased a big farm tractor and a chisel plow, intent on providing custom tillage to area farmers. Having been raised on beef, pork, and produce grown from Ontario County loam, my plan felt like a good fit.

I visited the same dealership where my dad's 7020 John Deere had come from, back in the day. Through a satellite dealership, some 40 miles away, they hooked me up with the biggest John Deere tractor made. This massive machine is a 9570 R with a Cummins engine rated at 570 horsepower. The purchase price, a mere $450,000. A price increase 2000% above that paid by my father, when he'd purchased the biggest John Deere tractor of his time. How ironic that it would take me a half-century to come back to where I first started, in the seat of a "Big Green Tractor."

With much remorse, Dad never got to see it working in the field. The very day my brother and I had moved the tractor and plow to work ground for the first time, I learned that he had fallen in his home and broken a hip. I had planned to pick him up the following morning, taking him to the field, so I might see the expression on his face when those 570 horses hit the ground. I regret that the day never happened. Dad passed away after waiting two weeks for surgery. Though things didn't go as planned, life goes on. I'm confident that he's keeping a watchful eye on me and the acres I'm covering, despite his physical absence.

My life has been a hell of a ride. If I had to do it all over again, I don't think I would change much along the way. My parents were part of our lives for many years, and I will cherish those memories forever. My beautiful wife is still the woman I love. I can't imagine having gone on this journey without her. We have been married for 45 years, and the best is yet to come. Our three children all live within ten miles of our home. We have been blessed with six grandchildren, five basketball players in the works, and one cheerleader to keep them all in control.

I can finally relax long enough to enjoy a vacation for the first time in my life. My wife and I purchased a townhouse on the ocean down South for the two of us, our children and grandkids to enjoy. It has become a perfect getaway. Our only need for a cell phone now comes when taking pictures of the dolphins circling about below. We still own our properties in New York but plan to travel south every chance we get. We are both 65 years young, healthy, and plan on enjoying the fruits of our labor for years to come.

While part of our success came from luck, perhaps divine intervention, it was our hard work and determination, which paid off. Our journey had brought me home.